The New Illustrated

Disney

SONGBOOK

Foreword by Steven Spielberg

Hal Leonard Publishing Corporation,
Milwaukee, Wisconsin

The New Illustrated

Disney

SONGBOOK

Harry N. Abrams, Inc.,
Publishers, New York

Project Manager: Lois Brown
Designer: Darilyn Lowe

For Hal Leonard Publishing Corporation: Glenda Herro, Managing Editor, Book Division

Music engraving by Hal Leonard Publishing Corporation, Milwaukee, Wisconsin

Library of Congress Cataloging-in-Publication Data
The new illustrated Disney songbook.

   1. vocal score.
   For voice and piano.
   Summary: Presents in sheet music format about
eighty songs from such Walt Disney movies as
"Cinderella," "Dumbo," and "Mary Poppins."
   1. Children's songs.   2. Moving-picture music—
Excerpts—Vocal scores with piano. [1. Songs. 2. Motion
picture music]   I. Disney, Walt, 1901–1966.   II. Walt
Disney Productions.
M1997.N437   1986   86-750676
ISBN 0-8109-0846-8 (Abrams)
ISBN 0-88188-467-7 (Hal Leonard)

Times Mirror Books

Printed and bound in Italy

Contents

 # Foreword

Walt Disney, whom I like to think of as the surrogate father of the "baby boomer" generation, was a man of indisputable wisdom and vision. He also possessed a remarkable ear for selecting music—both as to how it would work in his films and as to the types of songs that would invariably appeal to the American public at large.

I can't think of a single animated Disney feature that doesn't immediately associate itself with a song, nor can I think of a Disney song that doesn't inspire instant recognition of the Disney film from which it originated.

Beyond the technical problems of integrating music and film that Walt and his staff wrestled with and solved, I believe his greatest achievement was elevating music beyond its earlier role of mere accompaniment to the screen action. The perfection of the synchronization of music and movement, particularly in the cartoons of the thirties, serves as a symbol of the era of American craftsmanship.

Above all, Walt emphasized a sort of wistful optimism in his films, which I believe contributed to the American audience's perception of Disney films as the place where dreams and their fulfillment were within the reach of all dreamers. The word "dream" in relation to Walt Disney has probably been overused, but I think it illustrates that Walt was vitally aware that by appealing to people's strong desire to wish and dream, he would always have a central connection where it counted most . . . in their hearts.

The "baby boomers" did not necessarily grow up whistling the magnificent themes of Rodgers and Hammerstein, or Ira and George Gershwin. We had the music and lyrics memorized from "Give a Little Whistle," "Zip-A-Dee-Doo-Dah," "Bibbidi-Bobbidi-Boo," "When You Wish upon a Star," "Supercalifragilisticexpialidocious," and even though Ned Washington, Leigh Harline, Ray Gilbert, Allie Wrubel, Mack David, Al Hoffman, Jerry Livingston, Richard Sherman, and Robert Sherman were not generally thought of as household names, their music touched our hearts and gave us the songs of our earliest memories that we and our children must never forget.

Steven Spielberg
March 6, 1986

The New Illustrated

Disney

SONGBOOK

Heigh-Ho

From Walt Disney's
Snow White and the Seven Dwarfs

Words by Larry Morey
Music by Frank Churchill

ain't a bet-ter thing than a tune, Than a tune, You can whis - tle

or can croon. _____ "Heigh - Ho," "Heigh-
Ho," "Heigh-

Refrain

I'm Wishing

From Walt Disney's
Snow White and the Seven Dwarfs

Words by Larry Morey
Music by Frank Churchill

Slowly

I'm wish-ing _____ for the one I love to

find me _____ to-day. _____ I'm hop-ing, _____

_____ And I'm dream-ing of the nice things, _____ he'll

say. _____ Tell me, Wish-ing Well, _____ Will my wish come true? _____

_____ With your mag-ic spell, _____ Won't you tell my loved one what to

do? I'm wish-ing _____ for the one I

love to find me _____ to - day. _____

One Song

From Walt Disney's
Snow White and the Seven Dwarfs

Words by Larry Morey
Music by Frank Churchill

With a song I come to you, Like a trou-ba-dour, With a sim-ple ser-e-nade,

That, and noth-ing more. I have no lute to play. No tink-ling gui-tar.

Just a song to tell you, How sweet to me you are. One song, I have but

19

Some Day My Prince Will Come

From Walt Disney's
Snow White and the Seven Dwarfs

Words by Larry Morey
Music by Frank Churchill

Some day my prince will come, Some
day I'll find my love, And how thrilling that moment will
be, When the Prince of my dreams comes to me.

Some day I'll find my love, Some
one to call my own, And I'll know her the moment we
meet, For my heart will start skipping a beat.

Whistle While You Work

From Walt Disney's
Snow White and the Seven Dwarfs

Words by Larry Morey
Music by Frank Churchill

Brightly

Just whis - tle while you work. (whistle)
hum a mer - ry tune. (hum)

Put on that grin and start right in, To whis - tle loud and
Just do your best and then take a rest, And sing your - self a

long. Just song. When there's too much to do, Don't

With a Smile and a Song

From Walt Disney's *Snow White and the Seven Dwarfs*

Words by Larry Morey
Music by Frank Churchill

Lyrics:

With a smile and a song, Life is just like a bright sun-ny day, Your cares fade a-way, And your heart is young.

With a smile and a song, All the world seems to wak-en a-new, Re-joic-ing with you, As the song is sung.

There's no use in grum-bling, When rain-drops come tum-bling, Re-mem-ber you're the one, Who can fill the world with sun-shine. When you smile and you sing, Ev-'ry-thing is in tune and it's Spring and Life flows a-long,_____ With a smile and a song._____

Minnie's Yoo Hoo

Words by Walt Disney and Carl Stalling
Music by Carl Stalling

I'm the guy they call lit-tle Mick-ey Mouse, Got a sweet-ie down in the
blue bird down in the cher-ry tree, And the bu-sy buzz of the

chick-en house, Neith-er fat nor skin-ny, She's the hors-es whin-ny She's my
bum-ble bee, Eve-ning bells a-ring-in', Whip-poor-wills a-sing-in' Well they

27

bow, wow, wow, The crows caw, caw, and the mule's hee - haw Gosh what a rack - et like an

old buzz saw, I have list - ened to the Koo - koo kook his koo - koo, And I've

heard the roos - ter cock his doo - dle doo doo, With the cows and the chick - ens, they all

sound like the dick - ens, When I hear my lit - tle Min - nie's yoo hoo. Oh the yoo hoo.

The World Owes Me a Living

From Walt Disney's Silly Symphony,
The Grasshopper and the Ants

Words by Larry Morey
Music by Leigh Harline

There once was an old grass - hop - per who could on - ly think of fun, He looked on work as some - thing too un - pleas - ant to be done. He loved to sit in the sum - mer sun and fid - dle all day long. While doz - ing there he'd play this air, And

Copyright © 1934 Bourne Co. Copyright Renewed. This arrangement Copyright © 1979 Bourne Co.
Made in U.S.A.   International Copyright Secured   All Rights Reserved

sing this lit-tle song. "Oh the world owes me a liv-ing, Dee-dle, die-dle, doe-dle-die-dle

dum, Oh, the world owes me a liv-ing, Dee-dle, die-dle, doe-dle-die-dle

dum. If I worked hard all day. I must sleep bet-ter when in

bed at night, I sleep all day so that's all right, Dee-dle, die-dle, doe-dle-die-dle dum.

31

Who's Afraid of the Big Bad Wolf?

From Walt Disney's *Three Little Pigs*

Words and Music by Frank Churchill
Additional lyric by Ann Ronell

Lively

Who's a-fraid of the big bad wolf, big bad wolf, big bad wolf?

Who's a-fraid of the big bad wolf Tra-la-la-la-la. la. Long a-

go there were three pigs, lit-tle hand-some pig-gy-wigs, For the big bad, ver-y big

ver-y bad___ wolf, they___ did-n't give three figs, Num-ber one was ver-y gay, and he

built his house with hay; With a hey hey toot, he blew on his flute and he played a-round all

day. Who's a-fraid of the big bad wolf, big bad wolf,

big bad wolf? Who's a-fraid of the big bad wolf? Tra-la-la-la-la.

Give a Little Whistle

From Walt Disney's *Pinocchio*

Words by Ned Washington
Music by Leigh Harline

When you get in trou-ble and you don't know right from wrong;
When you meet temp-ta-tion, and the urge is ver-y strong;
Give a lit-tle whis-tle! (Whistle____) Give a lit-tle whis-tle! (Whistle____)
Not just a lit-tle squeak; Puck-er up and

Hi-Diddle-Dee-Dee (An Actor's Life For Me)

From Walt Disney's *Pinocchio*

Words by Ned Washington
Music by Leigh Harline

The grass is al-ways green-er in the oth-er fel-low's yard._____ No mat-ter what your life may be you think your life is hard_____ If we could pick and choose_____ and na-ture was-n't a

fac - tor, There's a bit of news ____ I'd pick the life of an act - or.

Hi - did - dle - dee - dee ____ An act - or's life for me ____ A high silk hat and a
Hi - did - dle - dee - dee ____ You sleep till af - ter two, ____ You prom - e - nade with a

sil - ver cane, A watch of gold with a dia - mond chain.
big cig - ar, You tour the world in a   pri - vate car, You

dine on chick - en and cav - i - ar, An act - or's life for me. ____

I've Got No Strings

From Walt Disney's *Pinocchio*

Words by Ned Washington
Music by Leigh Harline

I've got no strings to hold me down, To make me fret, or

make me frown, I had strings But now I'm free, There

are no strings on me. Hi o the

me - ri - o, I'm as hap - py as can be.

I want the world to know Noth-ing ev - er wor - ries me. I've

got no strings so I have fun, I'm not tied up to an - y - one,

How I love my li - ber - ty, There are no strings on me.

41

When You Wish upon a Star

From Walt Disney's *Pinocchio*

Words by Ned Washington
Music by Leigh Harline

Slowly, with expression

When you wish up-on a star, makes no diff-'rence
If your heart is in your dream,

who you are, An-y-thing your heart de-sires will
too ex-treme, When you wish up-on a star as

come to you.
dream-ers do. Fate is

Baby Mine

From Walt Disney's *Dumbo*

Words by Ned Washington
Music by Frank Churchill

Lyrics under the staves:

Ba - by mine _____ don't you cry _____
Lit - tle one _____ when you play _____

Ba - by mine _____ dry your eye _____
Don't you mind _____ what you say _____

Rest your head close to my heart, Nev - er to part, Ba - by of
Let those eyes spar - kle and shine, Nev - er a tear, Ba - by of

Casey Junior

From Walt Disney's *Dumbo*

Words by Ned Washington
Music by Frank Churchill

It's Cas - ey Jun - ior, com - in' down' the track _
Hear him puff - in' 'round the hill _

Com - in' down the track _ with a smok - y stack.
Cas - ey's here to thrill _ ev - 'ry Jack and Jill. _

Ev - 'ry time his fun - ny lit - tle

whis-tle sounds.___ (Toot toot) Ev-'ry-bo-dy hur-ries to the

Cir-cus Grounds.___ Time for lem-on-ade and

crack-er jack ___ Cas-ey Jun-ior's back,___ Cas-ey

Jun-ior's back a-gain.___

Pink Elephants on Parade

From Walt Disney's *Dumbo*

Words by Ned Washington
Music by Oliver Wallace

What a sight! Chase 'em a-way! Chase 'em a-way! I'm a-fraid

need your aid, Pink el-e-phants on pa-rade!_____

Repeat and fade out

Pink el-e-phants! Pink

When I See an Elephant Fly

From Walt Disney's *Dumbo*

Words by Ned Washington
Music by Oliver Wallace

Little April Shower

From Walt Disney's *Bambi*

Words by Larry Morey
Music by Frank Churchill

Drip, drip, drop, lit-tle A-pril show-er, beat-ing a tune as you fall all a-round.

Drip, drip, drop, lit-tle A-pril show-er, beat-ing a tune ev-'ry-where that you fall.

Drip, drip, drop, lit-tle A-pril show-er, what can com-pare with your beau-ti-ful sound.

Drip, drip, drop, lit-tle A-pril show-er, I'm get-ting wet and I don't care at all.

Drip, drip, drop, when the

To Coda

sky is cloud - y your pret - ty mu - sic can bright - en the day.

Drip, drip, drop, when the sun says, "How - dy" you say "Good-bye" right a - way. _____

D.C. al Coda

⊕ CODA

Drip! Drop! Drip! Drop! I'll nev - er be a - fraid of a

good lit - tle gay lit - tle A - pril ser - e - nade. _____

Love Is a Song

From Walt Disney's *Bambi*

Words by Larry Morey
Music by Frank Churchill

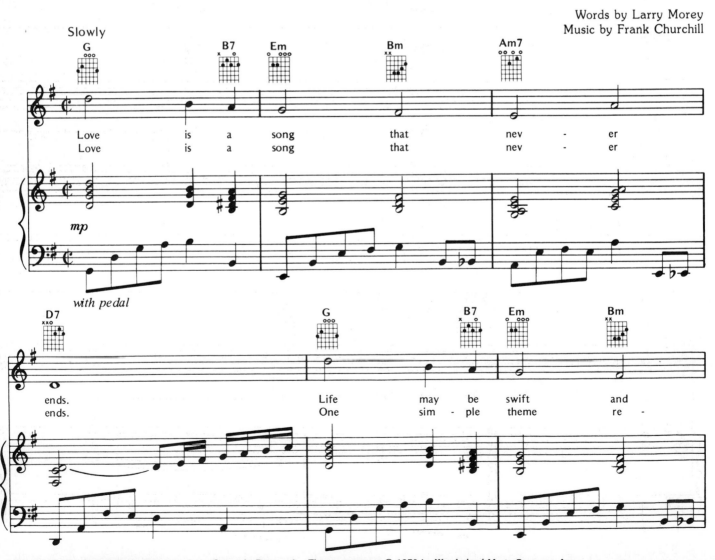

Zip-A-Dee-Doo-Dah

From Walt Disney's *Song of the South*

Words by Ray Gilbert
Music by Allie Wrubel

Merrily

Zip - a-dee-doo - dah, Zip - a-dee - ay, _____ My, oh

my, _____ what a won - der-ful day! _____ Plen - ty of sun - shine,

head - in' my way, _____ Zip - a-dee-doo - dah,

60

61

Lavender Blue
(Dilly Dilly)

From Walt Disney's *So Dear to My Heart*

Words by Larry Morey
Music by Eliot Daniel

Great grand-fa-ther met great grand-moth-er when she was a shy young miss, And great grand-fa-ther won great grand-moth-er with words more or less like this.

Lav - en - der blue dil - ly, dil - ly lav - en - der green;

If {I/you} were king, dil-ly, dil-ly {I'd/you'd} need a queen.

Who told me so, dil-ly, dil-ly, who told me so?

I told my-self, dil-ly, dil-ly, I told you so. If your

dil-ly, dil-ly heart feels a dil-ly, dil-ly way 'n if you'll an-swer "yes" In a

Blue Shadows
on the Trail

From Walt Disney's *Melody Time*

Words by Johnny Lange
Music by Eliot Daniel

Blue shad - ows on the trail,

Blue moon shin - ing through the trees, And a plain - tive

wail from the dis - tance comes a - drift - in' on the

The Lord Is Good to Me

From Walt Disney's *Melody Time*

Words and Music by Kim Gannon
and Walter Kent

68

do-in' as I please   sing-in' with my feath-ered friends,   Hum-min' with the

bees   I wake up ev-'ry day   as hap-py as can

be   be-cause I know that with His care my ap-ple trees they will

still be there, Oh the Lord's been good to   me. (whistle)

A Dream Is a Wish Your Heart Makes

From Walt Disney's *Cinderella*

Words and Music by
Mack David, Al Hoffman and Jerry Livingston

A dream is a wish your heart makes____ When you're fast a - sleep.____ In dreams you will lose your heart - aches;____ What - ev - er you wish for, you

Bibbidi-Bobbidi-Boo
(The Magic Song)

From Walt Disney's *Cinderella*

Words by Jerry Livingston
Music by Mack David and Al Hoffman

Brightly

Sa - la - ga - doo - la men - chic - ka boo - la

bib - bi - di - bob - bi - di - boo   Put 'em to - geth - er and what have you got   bib - bi - di - bob - bi - di - boo.

Sa - la - ga - doo - la men - chic - ka boo - la   bib - bi - di bob - bi - di - boo.   It - 'll do mag - ic be - lieve it   or not,

74

So This Is Love
(The Cinderella Waltz)

From Walt Disney's *Cinderella*

Words and Music by
Mack David, Al Hoffman and Jerry Livingston

So this is love, Mm_____ So this is love _____ So this is what makes life di - vine. _____ I'm all a - glow, Mm_____ And now I know _____ The key to all heav - en is

The Work Song

From Walt Disney's *Cinderella*

Words and Music by
Mack David, Al Hoffman and Jerry Livingston

Lyrics under the staves:

Cin-der-el-la, Cin-der-el-la, All I hear is Cin-der-el-la, from the mo-ment that I get up, till shades of night are fall-ing, There is-n't an-y let-up, I hear them call-ing,

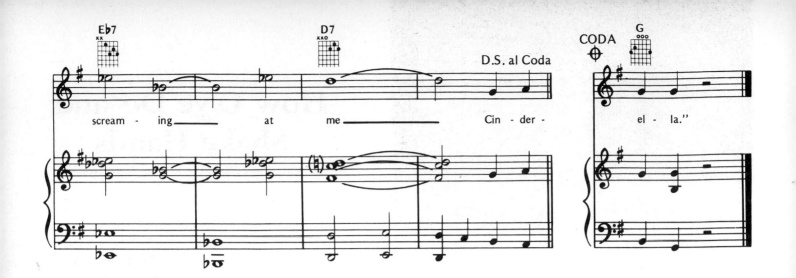

scream - ing ___ at me ___ Cin - der -   el - la."

How D'ye Do and Shake Hands

From Walt Disney's *Alice in Wonderland*

Words by Cy Coben
Music by Oliver Wallace

bus - 'ness.

2. You bus - 'ness.

3. You take your girl friend on a date and you have so much fun
That you forget to bring her home until it's after one,
Her father's waiting at the door as angry as can be,
I've had that happen lots of times, so take this tip from me, say: *(Refrain)*

4. While at the wedding of some folks you hardly know by sight,
And in a conversation with a woman on your right
You say you think the bride's a mess, her face she ought to hide,
And when you find you're talking to the mother of the bride, say:
(Refrain)

5. While walking thru a cemetery very late at night
You find that you're confronted by a figure dressed in white,
And tho the blood inside your veins has quickly turned to ice
Everything will be O.K. if you take my advice, say: *(Refrain)*

6. You walk into a restaurant as hungry as can be,
And when you've had a meal of ev'rything from A to Z
You realize you haven't got a single cent with you
And when the manager comes over this is what you do, say: *(Refrain)*

7. You're speeding down the highway and the feeling is superb,
And then you hear a siren and "Pull over to the curb,"
And when a cop who's big and tough comes walking up to you
And asks you where the fire is that you are going to, say: *(Refrain)*

8. You go into a barbershop to get yourself a shave,
And if you are the kind of guy who never can behave
You ask the manicurist for a little kiss or two
And then when you discover it's her husband shaving you, say: *(Refrain)*

*Always end A handshake and a happy greeting's mighty hard to beat,
with this   So at the risk of boring you I'm going to repeat
Verse   Remember in the future that no matter what you do
           Here's one way to get out of any mess you get into, say: *(Refrain)*

I'm Late

From Walt Disney's *Alice in Wonderland*

Words by Bob Hilliard
Music by Sammy Fain

Brightly

I'm late, I'm late for a ver-y im-por-tant date. No time to say hel-lo, good-bye, I'm late, I'm late, I'm late, I'm late and when I wave, I lose the time I save. My fuz-zy ears and

whis-kers took me too much time to shave. I run and then I hop, hop, hop, I

wish that I could fly. There's dan-ger if I dare to stop and

here's the rea-son why, (you see) I'm o-ver-due, I'm in a rab-bit

stew, Can't e-ven say good-bye, hel-lo, I'm late, I'm late, I'm late.

87

The Unbirthday Song

From Walt Disney's *Alice in Wonderland*

Words and Music by
Mack David, Al Hoffman and Jerry Livingston

Following the Leader

From Walt Disney's *Peter Pan*

Words by Ted Sears and Winston Hibler
Music by Oliver Wallace

Lyrics:

Fol-low-ing the lead-er, the lead-er, the lead-er, we're fol-low-ing the lead-er wher-ev-er he may go. ____ We won't be home till morn-ing, till morn-ing, till morn-ing, We

won't be home till morn - ing be - cause he told us so.   Tee

dum,   Tee   dee,   A   tee - dle ee dō tee day.   We're
dum,   Tee   dee,   A   tee - dle ee dō tee day.   We

out   for   fun   and   this is the game   we   play,   Come
march   a - long   and   these are the words   we   say,   Tee

on,   join   in   and   sing   your   trou - bles   a -
dum   Tee   dee   a   tee - dle   dee - dle   dee -

way, with a tee-dle ee dum a tee-dle ee dō tee
ay, oh, a tee-dle ee dum a tee-dle ee dō tee

day. We're day. Oh a

tee-dle ee dum a tee-dle ee dō tee day.

Never Smile at a Crocodile

From Walt Disney's *Peter Pan*

Words by Jack Lawrence
Music by Frank Churchill

Moderately slow

Ne-ver smile at a croc-o-dile, No, you can't get friend-ly with a croc-o-dile, Don't be

tak-en in by his wel-come grin, He's im-ag-in-ing how well you'd fit with-in his skin.

Nev-er smile at a croc-o-dile, Nev-er tip your hat and stop to talk a while { Nev-er
Don't be

The Second Star to the Right

From Walt Disney's *Peter Pan*

Words by Sammy Cahn
Music by Sammy Fain

98

Twin - kle, twin - kle lit - tle star so I'll know where you are,

Gleam - ing in the skies a - bove, lead me to the one who loves me,

And when you bring him my way each time we say "Good - night,"

we'll thank the lit - tle star that shines the sec - ond from the right.

You Can Fly!
You Can Fly!
You Can Fly!

From Walt Disney's *Peter Pan*

Words by Sammy Cahn
Music by Sammy Fain

Moderately

Think of the pres-ents you've brought
When there's a smile in your heart

An-y mer-ry lit-tle thought
There's no bet-ter time to start

Think of Christ-mas, think of snow,
It's a ver-y sim-ple plan.

Think of sleigh bells Here we go! Like
You can do what bird-ies can; At

rein-deer in the sky
least it's worth a try

You can fly! You can

To Coda

Mickey Mouse March

From Walt Disney's TV Series *Mickey Mouse Club*

Words and Music by Jimmie Dodd

Bella Notte

From Walt Disney's *Lady and the Tramp*

Words and Music by Peggy Lee
and Sonny Burke

This ___ is the night, ___ It's a beau - ti - ful night ___ And we

call it Bel - la Not - te. Look ___ at the skies; ___ They have

stars ___ in their eyes ___ On this love - ly Bel - la Not - te. So

He's a Tramp

From Walt Disney's *Lady and the Tramp*

Words and Music by Peggy Lee
and Sonny Burke

Lyrics:

He's a tramp, but they love him;_____ Breaks a new heart _____ ev-'ry
tramp, he's a scoun-drel,_____ He's a round-er, _____ he's a

day. He's a tramp; they a-dore him_____ And I on-ly hope he'll stay that
cad, He's a tramp, but I love him._____ Yes,_____

way. He's a ev-en I have got it pret-ty bad. You can nev-er tell when

8va
lower

La-La-Lu

From Walt Disney's *Lady and the Tramp*

Words and Music by Peggy Lee
and Sonny Burke

Lyrics:

La - la - lu, la - la - lu, Oh, my lit - tle star sweep - er,
lu, la - la - lu, Lit - tle wan - der - ing an - gel,

I'll sweep the star - dust for you.

La - la - lu, la - la - lu, Lit - tle soft, fluff - y

The Siamese Cat Song

From Walt Disney's *Lady and the Tramp*

Words and Music by Peggy Lee
and Sonny Burke

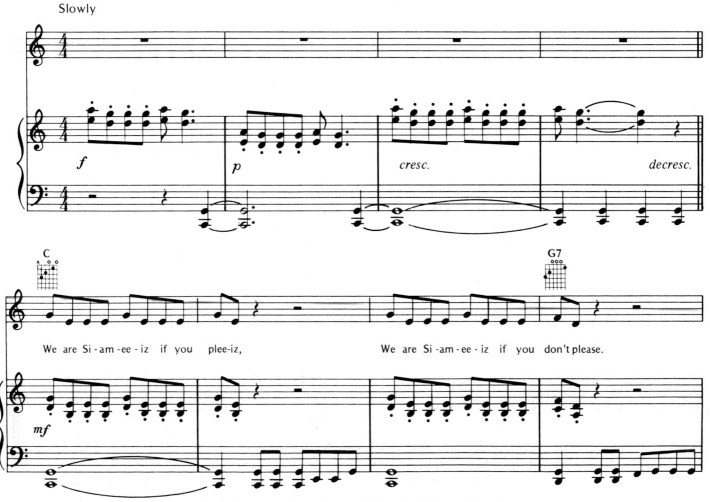

We are Si-am-ee-iz if you plee-iz,

We are Si-am-ee-iz if you don't please.

The Ballad of Davy Crockett

From Walt Disney's Television Production *Davy Crockett*

Words by Tom Blackburn
Music by George Bruns

Born on a moun-tain top in Ten - nes - see, Green - est state in the Land of the Free. Raised in the woods so's he knew ev -'ry tree Kilt him a b'ar when he was on - ly three. Da - vy, Da - vy Crock-ett,

King of the wild fron - tier! In eight-een — thir - teen the Creeks up - rose, add-in' red-skin ar - rows to the coun - try's — woes. Now In - jun fight - in' is some - thin' he knows so he shoul - ders his ri - fle an' off he — goes.

Chorus

Da - vy, Da - vy Crock - ett, the man who don't know fear!

Wringle Wrangle
(A Pretty Woman's Love)

From Walt Disney's *Westward Ho the Wagons!*

Words and Music by Stan Jones

Lively

Oh   Oh   Wrin - gle, wran - gle   jing - a - jong jan - gle

(whistle) Hey! (slap leg) A might-y fine horse I'm in love of course 'cause I got me a pret-ty wo-man's

love.   Oh love.   With a dol-lars worth of beans, a new pair of jeans, got a

Once Upon a Dream

(Based on the *Sleeping Beauty* Theme)
From Walt Disney's *Sleeping Beauty*

Words and Adaptation of Music by
Sammy Fain and Jack Lawrence

Let's Get Together

From Walt Disney's *The Parent Trap*

Words and Music by Richard M. Sherman
and Robert B. Sherman

Moderate rock tempo

Let's get to-geth-er Yea, yea yea!__ Why don't you and I com - bine?__ / Think of all that we could share.__

Let's get to-gether What do you say?__ / Ev - 'ry day,__ We could have a swing-in' time.__ We'd be a / Ev - 'ry way and ev - 'ry - where.__ And tho' we

cra - a - zy team Why don't we ma - a - ake the scene To- / have - n't got a lot, We could be shar - in' all we got To-

geth-er.____ Oh!____

geth-er.____ Oh, I real-ly

think you're swell.__ Uh huh, we real-ly ring the bell. Ooh____ ee, and if you

stick with me,__ Noth-in' could be great-er. Say, hey, al-li-ga-tor! Let's get to-geth-er

Yea, yea yea!__ Two is twice as nice as one.__ Let's get to-geth-er.

121

Right ___ a - way, ___ We'll be hav - in' twice the fun, ___ And you can al - ways count on me, A groov - y two - some we will be. Let's get to - geth - er. ___ Yea, yea, yea! ___

Toyland March

From Walt Disney's
Babes in Toyland

Words by Mel Leven
Music by George Bruns
Adapted from a Victor Herbert Melody

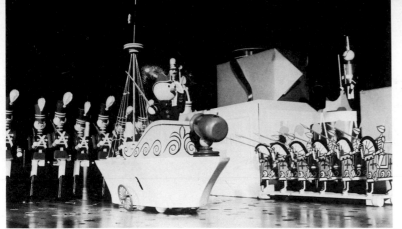

Lyrics:

Toy - land, toy - land, Dear lit - tle girl and boy land, While you dwell with -
Toy - land, toy - land, We're on our way to toy - land, Don't know when we'll

in it You are ev - er hap - py there. Child - hood's toy - land, Won - der - ful world of
get there, But we know there's fun in store. Toy - land, toy - land, Won - der - ful girl and

joy land, Would - n't it be fine if we could stay there for - ev - er more.
boy land, Once you leave its bor - ders you can nev - er re - turn a - gain.

Cruella de Ville

From Walt Disney's *101 Dalmatians*

Words and Music by Mel Leven

Slow Blues

Cru-el-la de Ville,— Cru-el-la de Ville,— if she does-n't scare you no
curl of her lips,— the ice in her stare;— all in-no-cent chil-dren had

e-vil thing will.— To see her is to take a sud-den chill,— Cru-el-la, Cru-el-la de
bet-ter be-ware.— She's like a spi-der wait-ing for the kill,— Cru-

Ville. The el-la, Cru-el-la de Ville. At first you think Cru-el-la is the

Chim Chim Cher-ee

From Walt Disney's *Mary Poppins*

Words and Music by Richard M. Sherman
and Robert B. Sherman

Chim chim-in-ey, chim chim-in-ey, chim chim cher-ee! A sweep is as luck-y as luck-y can be. Chim chim-in-ey,

Up where the smoke is all bill-ered and curled, 'Tween pave-ment and stars is the chim-ney sweep world. When there's 'ard-ly no

you're with a sweep you're in glad com - pa - ny!

No - where is there a more 'ap - pi - er crew Than

them wot sings chim chim cher - ee, chim cher - oo!

Chim chim - in - ey chim chim cher - ee, chim cher - oo!

Feed the Birds
(Tuppence a Bag)
From Walt Disney's *Mary Poppins*

Words and Music by Richard M. Sherman
and Robert B. Sherman

Feed _____ the birds, tup - pence _____ a bag,

Tup - pence, _____ tup - pence, _____ tup - pence _____ a bag.

"Feed _____ the birds," that's what she cries

time some-one shows that he cares. _____ Though ____ her

words are sim-ple ____ and few, Lis-ten, ____ lis-ten ____ she's

cal-ling to you. "Feed ____ the birds, tup-pence ____ a

bag, Tup-pence, ____ tup-pence, ____ tup-pence a bag."

I Love to Laugh

From Walt Disney's *Mary Poppins*

Words and Music by Richard M. Sherman
and Robert B. Sherman

Let's Go Fly a Kite

From Walt Disney's *Mary Poppins*

Words and Music by Richard M. Sherman
and Robert B. Sherman

Let's go fly a kite
up to the high-est height!
Let's go fly a kite and

136

send   it   soar - ing   up   through   the   at - mos - phere,   Up   where   the   air   is   clear.   Oh,   let's   go _____ fly   a   kite!   Let's   go   fly   a   kite. _____

A Spoonful of Sugar

From Walt Disney's *Mary Poppins*

Words and Music by Richard M. Sherman
and Robert B. Sherman

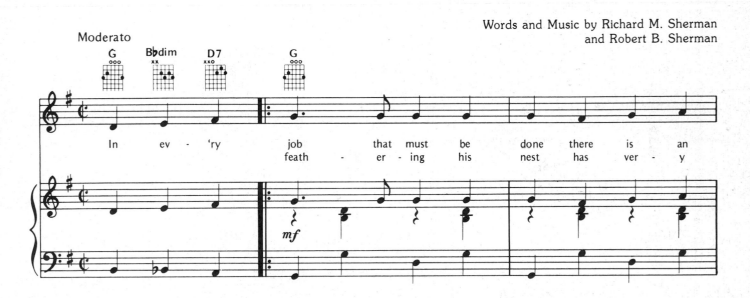

In ev - 'ry job that must be done there is an
feath - er - ing his nest has ver - y

el - e - ment of fun; You find the fun and
lit - tle time to rest While find gath - er - ing his

139

snap the job's a game; _____ And ev-'ry task you un-der-
bits of twine and twig. _____ Though quite in-tent in his pur-

take be-comes a piece of cake, A lark! A
suit he has a mer-ry tune to toot; He knows a

spree! It's ver-y clear to see That a
song will move the job a-long For a

spoon-ful of su-gar helps the med-i-cine go

down, The med - i - cine go dow - wown,

med - i - cine go down. Just a spoon - ful of

sug - ar helps the med - i - cine go down In a most de -

light - ful way. _____ A rob - in way. _____

141

Step In Time

From Walt Disney's *Mary Poppins*

Words and Music by Richard M. Sherman
and Robert B. Sherman

Lyrics:

Kick your knees up, step in time! Kick your knees up, step in time! Nev-er need a rea-son, nev-er need a rhyme,
Spin a-bout and step in time! Spin a-bout and step in time! Nev-er need a rea-son, nev-er need a rhyme,

Kick your knees up, step in time! Link your el-bows, step in time! Link your el-bows,
Spin a-bout and step in time! 'Round the chim-ney, step in time! 'Round the chim-ney,

step in time! Nev-er need a rea-son, nev-er need a rhyme, Link your el-bows, step in time!
step in time! Nev-er need a rea-son, nev-er need a rhyme, 'Round the chim-ney, step in time!

Flap like a bird - ie,
Step in time,

step in time! Flap like a bird-ie, step in time! Nev-er need a rea-son, nev-er need a rhyme,
step in time, Step in time, step in time! Nev-er need a rea-son, nev-er need a rhyme, When you

Flap like a bird - ie, step in time! step in time, you step in time!

Supercalifragilisticexpialidocious

From Walt Disney's *Mary Poppins*

Words and Music by Richard M. Sherman
and Robert B. Sherman

E - ven though the sound of it is some - thing quite a - tro - cious!
Sup - er - cal - i - frag - il - is - tic - ex - pi - al - i - do - cious!

If 'you say it loud e - nough, you'll al - ways sound pre - co - cious.
Sup - er - cal - i - frag - il - is - tic - ex - pi - al - i - do - cious.

Sup - er - cal - i - frag - il - is - tic - ex - pi - al - i - do - cious!
Sup - er - cal - i - frag - il - is - tic - ex - pi - al - i - do - cious!

Um did -dle did -dle did -dle, um did -dle ay! Um did -dle did -dle did -dle um did -dle ay! { Be -
So

145

It's a Small World

Theme from the Disneyland and Walt Disney
World Attraction, *It's a Small World*

Words and Music by Richard M. Sherman
and Robert B. Sherman

It's a world of laugh - ter, a world of tears; it's a
just one moon and one gold - en sun and a

world of hopes and a world of fears. There's so
smile of means friend - ship to ev - 'ry one, Though the

much that we share that it's time we're a - ware. It's a
moun - tains di - vide and the o - ceans are wide, It's a

Winnie the Pooh

From Walt Disney's
Winnie the Pooh and the Honey Tree

Words and Music by Richard M. Sherman
and Robert B. Sherman

and there's Owl, but most of all Win - nie the Pooh!

Win - nie the Pooh, Win - nie the Pooh, tub - by lit - tle cub - by all

stuffed with fluff, He's Win - nie the Pooh, Win - nie the Pooh;

wil - ly, nil - ly, sil - ly ole bear. bear.

The Bare Necessities

From Walt Disney's *The Jungle Book*

Words and Music by Terry Gilkyson

Look for the bare ne-ces-si-ties, the sim-ple bare ne-ces-si-ties,_ for-get a-bout your wor-ries and your strife. I mean the bare ne-ces-si-ties_ or Moth-er Na-ture's re-ci-pes_ that

I Wan'na Be
Like You
(The Monkey Song)

From Walt Disney's *The Jungle Book*

Words and Music by Richard M. Sherman
and Robert B. Sherman

man - cub,   And   stroll   right   in - to   town,   and
man - cub,   Just   clue   me   what   to   do,   give

be   just   like   the   oth - er   men,   I'm   tired   of   mon - key - in'
me   the   pow'r   of   man's   red   flow'r,   and   make   my   dream___ come

'round!
true!

Oh   Ooh,   ooh,   oh!   (Ee - ee)   I   wan - na   be   like

you,   ooh,   ooh!   (Ee - ee)   I   wan - na   walk   like   you,

158

Fortuosity

From Walt Disney's *The Happiest Millionaire*

Words and Music by Richard M. Sherman
and Robert B. Sherman

clo - vers are found.___   For - tu - os - i - ty,   luck - y
just wait and see.___   For - tu - os - i - ty,   luck - y

chanc - es.   For - tu - i -tious lit - tle   hap - py   hap - pen-stan - ces.
chanc - es.   For - tu - i -tious lit - tle   hap - py   hap - pen-stan - ces.

I   don't   wor - ry   'cause   ev - 'ry - where I   see   that
I   keep   smil - in'   'cause   my phil - os - o - phy   is

ev - 'ry bit   of   life is lit   by   for - tu - os - i - ty!
"Do your best and   leave the rest   to   for - tu - os - i - ty!"

161

Yo, Ho
(A Pirate's Life for Me)

From Walt Disney's *Disneyland*

Words by Xavier Atencio
Music by George Bruns

In a robust manner

Yo ho, yo ho, a pi - rate's life for me. We
Yo ho, yo ho, a pi - rate's life for me. We
Yo ho, yo ho, a pi - rate's life for me. We

pil - lage, plun - der, we ri - fle and loot. Drink up me 'eart - ies, yo ho. We
ex - tort and pil - fer, we filch and sack. Drink up me 'eart - ies, yo ho. Ma -
kin - dle and char and in - flame and ig - nite. Drink up me 'eart - ies, yo ho. We

kid - nap and rav - age and don't give a hoot. Drink up me 'eart - ies, yo ho.
raud and em - bez - zle and e - ven high - jack. Drink up me 'eart - ies, yo ho.
burn up the cit - y, we're real - ly a fright. Drink

The Wonderful Thing about Tiggers

From Walt Disney's *Winnie the Pooh and the Blustery Day*

Words and Music by Richard M. Sherman
and Robert B. Sherman

Ev'rybody Wants to Be a Cat

From Walt Disney's *The Aristocats*

Words and Music by Floyd Huddleston
and Al Rinker

Ev-'ry-bod-y wants to be a cat, be-cause a cat's the on-ly cat who knows where it's at! __ Ev-'ry-bod-y pick-in' up on the fe-line beat, __ 'cause ev-'ry-thing else is ob-so-lete. Be-ware of a square __ when he of-fers to share __ his

Come on, scat cat, turn me on,__ I'll take my horn and my best tone,__ Then blow a lit- tle soul in-to the

tune.   Let's take it to an-oth-er key,__ Mod-u-late, then wait for me,__ I'll

take a few ad libs and pret-ty soon   The oth-er cats   will all com-mence__

con- gre-gat- ing on the fence,__ be - neath the al- ley's on-ly light,__ where ev- 'ry night is out   of sight!

D.C. al Fine

169

Scales and Arpeggios

From Walt Disney's *The Aristocats*

Words and Music by Richard M. Sherman
and Robert B. Sherman

Lyrics:

Ev-'ry tru-ly cul-tured mu-sic stu-dent knows, You must learn your scales and your ar - peg - gi - os.

Bring the mu-sic ring-ing from your chest and not your nose, While you sing your scales and your ar -

peg - gi - os. Do mi so do do so mi do If you're faith-ful to your dai-ly

prac - tic - ing, You will find your pro-gress is en - cour - ag - ing. Do mi so mi do mi so mi

fa la so it goes, When you do the scales and your ar - peg - gi - os.

Do mi so do do so mi do do mi so do do so mi do Train your-self to draw a line that's

straight and true, Then your brush will do just what you want it to.

If you stu - dy, you won't mud-dy up each bril - liant hue; Prac - tic-ing your paint-ing is the thing to do.

Do mi so do do so mi do do mi so do do so mi do Though at first it seems as tho' it does - n't show.

Like a tree, a - bil - i - ty will bloom and grow. If you're smart, you'll learn by heart what ev - 'ry art - ist knows:

Lines and col - ors, scales and your ar - peg - gi - os!

These Are the Best Times

From Walt Disney Productions' *Superdad*

Words and Music by Shane Tatum

These are the best times _____ the mo-ments we can't let slip _____ a-
But once in a life time _____ a min-ute like this is ours _____ to

way _____ life's lit-tle game _____ we play for liv-ing from day to
share re-mem-ber these mo - ments well for

day. _____ mo-ments like these are rare as dreams and

Love

From Walt Disney Productions' *Robin Hood*

Words by Floyd Huddleston
Music by George Bruns

Oo-De-Lally

From Walt Disney Productions' *Robin Hood*

Words and Music by Roger Miller

Moderately

Rob - in Hood and Lit - tle John walk-in' thru the for - est, Laugh-in' back and forth at what the
Rob - in Hood and Lit - tle John run-nin'thru the for - est, Jump-in' fen - ces dodg-in' trees and

oth-er 'un has to say. ____ Re - min - isc - in' this 'n that 'n
try-in' to get a - way. ____ Con-tem-pla - tin' noth-in' but es -

hav - in' such a good time. } Oo - de - lal - ly, Hoo-de-lal - ly, Gol - ly what a day! ____
cape and fin - 'ly makin' it.

Sweet Surrender

From Walt Disney Productions' *The Bears and I*

Words and Music by John Denver

Moderately slow

Lost and a-lone on some___ for-got-ten high-way,___ ___ tra-veled by man-y, re-mem-bered by few.___ Look-in' for some-thing that I can be-lieve in,___ look-in' for some-thing that

more than e-nough,___ just___ be here to-day,

and he don't know what___ the fu-ture is hold-in' in

store. I don't know where I'm go-in', I'm not sure where I've been.___

___ There's a spir-it that guides me,___ a

183

185

Someone's Waiting for You

From Walt Disney Productions' *The Rescuers*

Words by Carol Connors and Ayn Robbins
Music by Sammy Fain

Ev-'ry child has man-y wish-es that they wish when they're a-lone. Faith can work just like mag-ic; noth-ing chang-es when you're grown. Be brave lit-tle one Make a wish for each sad lit-tle tear

light.   Soon there'll be joy and hap - pi - ness and your lit - tle world will be

bright.   Have faith lit - tle one   'til your hopes and your wish - es come true

You must try to be brave lit - tle one_____ Some - one's wait - ing

to love you. _____

8va
lower

Candle
on the Water

From Walt Disney Productions' *Pete's Dragon*

Words and Music by Al Kasha
and Joel Hirschhorn

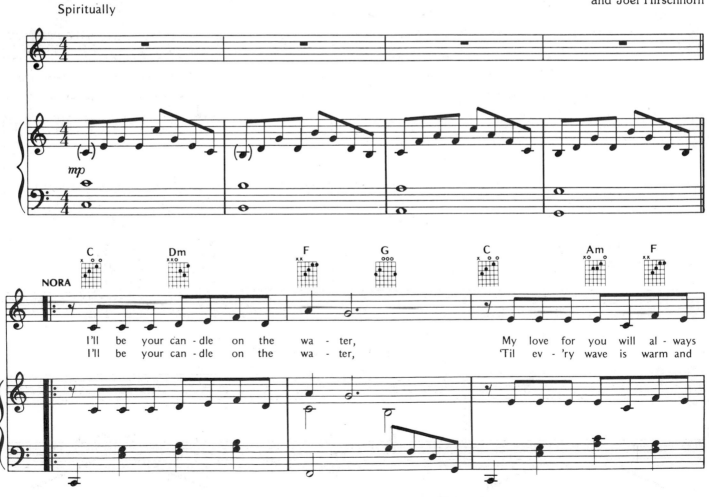

cir - cling in the air   light - ed by a   prayer.

I'll be your can - dle on the wa - ter,

this flame in - side of me will grow.   Keep hold - ing   on,   you'll make it,

Here's my hand so take it,   look for me reach - ing out to   show   as sure as riv - ers

flow, I'll nev-er let you go,

I'll nev-er let you go, I'll nev-er let you

go.

It's Not Easy

From Walt Disney Productions' *Pete's Dragon*

Words and Music by Al Kasha
and Joel Hirschhorn

Disco
Mickey Mouse

From Walt Disney Productions' *Mickey Mouse Disco*

Words and Music by Tom Worrall

Medium Disco Beat

He's a mov-ie star. ___
mach-o guy ___

The la-dies say he's sweet. ___ Well, his
with Clark Ga-ble ears. ___ When his

bod-y's got ___ the mo-tion, and the rhy-thm's in ___ his feet. ___
bod-y's set ___ in mo-tion, the la-dies cry a thou-sand tears. ___

Macho Duck

From Walt Disney Productions' *Mickey Mouse Disco*

Words and Music by Tom Worrall

Well, he's got style, __ and he's got flair, __ got two left feet __ but he does-n't care. __ Dressed in blue, __ fit to form; __ the la-dies love __ to touch his u - ni-form. __ Mess with him __ and you're out __ of luck. He's a ma-cho duck.

Additional verses

Can he move? Well, guess what?
He's got a wiggle and a waddle strut.
But feathers fly when he gets riled,
It's like a pillow fight that's gone wild.
Mess with him and you're out of luck.
He's a macho duck.

To Chorus

Builds his muscles, meets the test.
Gots lots of feathers on his chest.
He's laid back, he's in demand,
But he's really hard to understand.
Mess with him and you're out of luck.
He's a macho duck.

To Chorus

Best of Friends

From Walt Disney Productions'
The Fox and the Hound

Words by Stan Fidel
Music by Richard Johnston

When you're the best of friends _____ hav-ing so much fun to-geth-
hap-py game, _____ you could clown a-round for-ev-

-er, you're not e-ven a-ware ___ you're such a fun-ny pair. ___
-er. Nei-ther one of you sees ___ your nat-ur'l bound-a-ries. ___

You're the best ___ of friends. ___ Life's a Life's one hap-py game.

all that you dis-cov - er, when these mo - ments have passed__ will that

friend - ship last?__ Who can say __ if there's a way?__ How I hope,__

I hope it nev - er ends, _____ 'cause you're__ the

best of friends. _____

Happy Birthday

From Walt Disney Productions' *Splashdance*

Words by Michael Silversher
and Patricia Silversher
Music by Michael Silversher

Hap-py Birth-day, Hap-py Birth-day, Hap-py, Hap-py Birth-day to you.

Hap-py Birth-day, Hap-py Birth-day, Hap-py, Hap-py Birth-day to you.

I want to do some-thing spe-cial for you. It's your birth-day and you're spe-cial too,___ So
The grand-est pre-sent I've saved till the end, 'cause you're the best-est of all of my friends.___ Here's

209

Love Came for Me

From Walt Disney Productions' *Splash*

Words by Lee Holdridge
Music by Will Jennings

shin - ing in clear blue skies; _____ We flowed to - geth - er, _____

__ once and for - ev - er love came for me.

One fine night _____ love let us see

how far we'll go, how good we'll be.

213

 # Song Index